Hurricane

Perspectives on storm disasters

Andrew Langley

 Raintree

Raintree is an imprint of Capstone Global Library Limited, a company incorporated in England and Wales having its registered office at 7 Pilgrim Street, London, EC4V 6LB – Registered company number: 6695582

www.raintreepublishers.co.uk
myorders@raintreepublishers.co.uk

Edited by Andrew Farrow, James Benefield and Claire Throp
Designed by Philippa Jenkins
Original illustrations © Capstone Global Library Ltd 2014
Picture research by Tracy Cummins
Originated by Capstone Global Library Ltd
Printed in China

ISBN 978 1 406 28029 6
18 17 16 15 14
10 9 8 7 6 5 4 3 2 1

British Library Cataloguing in Publication Data
A full catalogue record for this book is available from the British Library.

Acknowledgements

We would like to thank the following for permission to reproduce photographs: Alamy p. 28 (© Dennis MacDonald); AP Photo p. 32 (Harry Koundakjian); Corbis pp. 4 (© Ken Cedeno), 17 (© Karsten Moran/Aurora Photos), 18 (© HANDOUT/Reuters), 27 (© Rick Friedman); DVIDS p. 44 (Petty Officer 2nd Class Erik Barker); Getty Images pp. 11 (Carl Juste/ Miami Herald/MCT), 14 (Andrew Burton), 23, 42 (STAN HONDA/AFP), 34, 37 (Joe Raedle), 40 (Justin Sullivan), 46 (ROBERTO SCHMIDT), 48 (Emile Wamsteker/Bloomberg); Newscom pp. 12 (EPA/JEAN JACQUES AGUSTIN), 21 (Zach Huff/Lightroom Photos/USCG); NOAA p. 31; U.S. Navy Photo p. 25 (Mass Communication Specialist 1st Class Emmitt J. Hawks); Wikimedia p. 39 (Roger Edson, University of Guam).

Cover photograph of the eyewall of Hurricane Jimena as it struck Puerto San Carlos on 2 September 2009, reproduced with permission of Science Source (Jim Edds).

Every effort has been made to contact copyright holders of material reproduced in this book. Any omissions will be rectified in subsequent printings if notice is given to the publisher.

Disclaimer
All the internet addresses (URLs) given in this book were valid at the time of going to press. However, due to the dynamic nature of the internet, some addresses may have changed, or sites may have changed or ceased to exist since publication. While the author and publisher regret any inconvenience this may cause readers, no responsibility for any such changes can be accepted by either the author or the publisher.

Contents

Some words are printed in bold, **like this**. You can find out what they mean by looking in the glossary.

DOSSIER:
HURRICANE SANDY

Hurricane Sandy was one of the biggest and deadliest Atlantic storms ever recorded, killing at least 147 people. It lasted just 10 days, from 22 October to 31 October 2012. Building in the Caribbean, Sandy swept northwards, causing wind damage, flooding and death in Jamaica, Cuba, Hispaniola and other islands. Then the hurricane landed on the north-eastern coast of the United States, its full force hitting the states of New Jersey and New York. Besides the ferocious winds, it created a massive surge of water, which flooded much of New York City. Hurricane Sandy brought mayhem to 24 US states, as well as parts of eastern Canada.

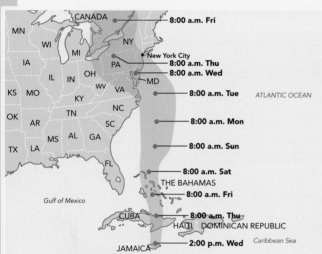

This map shows the track of Hurricane Sandy northwards from the Caribbean to its landfall in the north-eastern United States and eastern Canada.

Even giant tankers were helpless against the storm surge. Many were swept onto the coast and left grounded.

WIND SPEEDS:	highest wind speed in Caribbean: 184 km (114 mi.) per hour over Cuba. Highest speed over US land: 128 km (80 mi.) per hour
TOTAL AREA CROSSED:	5.18 million sq. km (2 million sq. mi.)
DEATHS:	285 (138 of these were from disease and other causes)
HOMES DESTROYED:	1,025,000 (of these, 650,000 were in the United States)
TOTAL COST:	estimated at $72 billion, making Sandy the second costliest Atlantic hurricane, after Katrina in 2005

HURRICANE SANDY TIMELINE

22 OCTOBER
A tropical **depression** (area of low air pressure) forms in the south-western Caribbean Sea. By 5.00 p.m. it has grown into a tropical storm, named Sandy.

24 OCTOBER
Sandy strengthens into a Category 1 hurricane, with winds of up to 128 km (80 mi.) per hour and moves north. It causes massive damage in Jamaica, and floods in Haiti and the Dominican Republic.

25 OCTOBER
Now a Category 2 hurricane, Sandy crosses eastern Cuba, damaging many houses and killing 11 people

26 OCTOBER
The hurricane tracks across the Bahamas, bringing more devastation

27 OCTOBER
Sandy briefly weakens to a tropical storm before strengthening again to Category 1. It turns north towards the US coast.

28 OCTOBER
The hurricane meets a cold weather system, which creates more energy and it starts to change into a **superstorm**

29 OCTOBER
Sandy makes landfall, striking New Jersey and New York. Its huge **storm surge** causes extensive flooding, while the winds fell trees and buildings.

Deadly storm

A hurricane like Sandy is one of the most gigantic and powerful natural events on Earth. This mass of rainclouds, thunderstorms and high winds may cover an area of many hundreds of square kilometres. The mass rotates around a central point called the eye. This is a calm area, usually about 32 kilometres (20 miles) wide, with much lighter winds.

The winds outside the eye may reach speeds of more than 250 kilometres (155 miles) per hour, enough to snap trees and destroy buildings. The clouds drop vast amounts of rain, creating **flash floods**. Wind and rain can also combine with tides to produce a storm surge, pushing huge waves onto coastlines.

The power of nature

"A tropical **cyclone** [hurricane] releases energy equivalent to a **hydrogen bomb** explosion every minute of its existence! These gigantic **vortices** [spirals] are responsible for more death and destruction than any other natural event."

John Whittow, British expert on geography and earth sciences

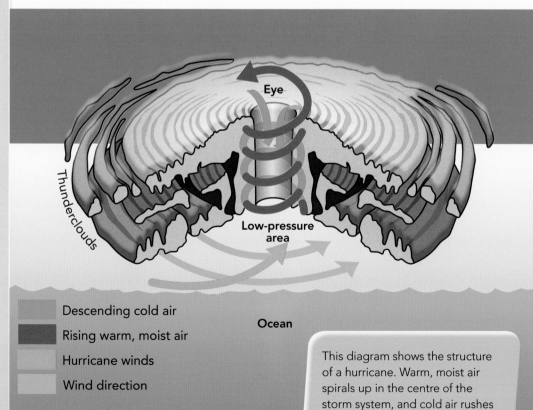

Eye

Thunderclouds

Low-pressure area

Ocean

Descending cold air

Rising warm, moist air

Hurricane winds

Wind direction

This diagram shows the structure of a hurricane. Warm, moist air spirals up in the centre of the storm system, and cold air rushes in to fill the gap below.

Speeding up: from depression to hurricane	
Type	Wind speed
Tropical depression	less than 61 km (38 mi.) per hour
Tropical storm	63–117 km (39–73 mi.) per hour
Hurricane	119 km (74 mi.) per hour or more
Major hurricane	170 km (111 mi.) per hour

(There are also different categories of hurricanes – see page 35.)

A hurricane is born

Hurricane Sandy's short and deadly life began in the same way most Atlantic Ocean hurricanes begin life. A long, thin region of low air pressure (see box below) moves out of the tropical region of the Atlantic east of the Caribbean. This is called a tropical depression, and it contains clouds and thunderstorms. The ocean warms this air, causing it to rise up. It takes with it water droplets, which evaporate in the warm air. Cooler, dryer air flows into the gap left by the evaporated water, causing powerful winds.

This moist air is funnelled into the sky. As it rises, the water in it changes from water vapour to water droplets, and heat is expelled into the surrounding air. Cooler air comes in to replace the rising air, but is warmed and then rises itself. Gradually, the wind speeds grow and the depression strengthens into a tropical storm.

Every year, hundreds of these storm systems come spinning out of the tropical regions of the world, just north and south of the **equator**. Most of them fade away without causing any significant damage. But some (usually between 40 and 50) grow in size and wind speed and become full-blown hurricanes. Sandy was one of them.

Air pressure

Air is not weightless. Gravity pulls the gases in the **atmosphere** towards Earth and presses them down on the surface. This creates air pressure. But this pressure is always changing. When the Sun heats the ocean or land, they pass this warmth to the air above them. When air is warmed, its **molecules** move further apart, it becomes less **dense** and its pressure drops. This low-pressure air rises (rather like a hot air balloon), and colder, higher pressure air rushes in to take its place.

The hurricane season

Nearly all hurricanes begin in the tropical regions on either side of the equator. These are the warmest and wettest parts of the world. There are seven hurricane areas, called **hurricane basins**. They are named after the three major oceans that cover the **tropics**. Major storms develop from the seven hurricane basins every year. Each basin has a slightly different hurricane season:

Hurricane basin	Season
Atlantic Ocean (including the North Atlantic, Gulf of Mexico, and Caribbean Sea)	1 June to 30 November
Pacific Ocean, north-east (from Mexico to the mid-Pacific)	15 May to 30 November
Pacific Ocean, north-west (from the mid-Pacific to Asia and the South China Sea)	No common start or end date, as storms are likely throughout the year
Pacific Ocean, south (from the mid-Pacific to Australia)	1 November to 30 April
Indian Ocean, north (including the Bay of Bengal and Arabian Sea)	April to June and September to early December
Indian Ocean, south-west (from Africa to the mid-Indian Ocean)	17 November to 20 April
Indian Ocean, south-east (from the South China Sea to Australia)	November to May

Why do hurricanes spin?

All hurricanes spin at enormous speeds. This spinning is created by the rotation of Earth, which makes large moving objects (such as storms and winds) veer off course and travel in a curve. This is called the Coriolis Force. In the Northern Hemisphere, the Coriolis Force causes winds to curve to the right. As a result, hurricanes turn anti-clockwise. In the Southern Hemisphere, the Coriolis Force pushes winds to the left. Here, hurricanes spin clockwise.

Hurricane hotspots

Some places suffer more than their fair share of hurricane strikes. In the Caribbean, Hurricane Sandy was just the latest in a long line of storms to strike the Bahamas. Some Bahamian islands have been hit by over 80 hurricanes since 1871 (when records began). On the east coast of the United States, North Carolina is most vulnerable. Cape Hatteras, for example, has seen over 100 hurricanes in the same period – even though Sandy gave it a miss in 2012.

Other areas around the world are especially at risk from these violent storms. The southern coast of China, the Philippines, Mexico, Japan and Australia have all been in the path of a large number of tropical cyclones. One of the worst-hit countries is Bangladesh, in Asia. Here, the winds drive huge storm surges up the Bay of Bengal, flooding vast areas of low-lying land. Since 1983, the country has been devastated by at least 14 major cyclones.

What's in a name?

The word "hurricane" is only used to describe storms in the North Atlantic and north-east Pacific. In the north-west Pacific, they are called **typhoons**. In the Southern Hemisphere and the Indian Ocean, they are simply called cyclones. However, the correct term, which is used by scientists, is "tropical cyclones".

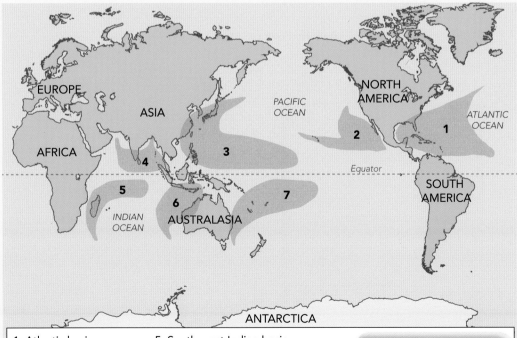

1. Atlantic basin
2. North-east Pacific basin
3. North-west Pacific basin
4. North Indian basin
5. South-west Indian basin
6. South-east Indian basin
7. Australian/South-west Pacific basin

This map shows the major basins in which tropical cyclones occur.

There's a storm coming

On 19 October 2012, Stacey R. Stewart was at work at the National Hurricane Center (NHC) in Miami, Florida. That evening, at 8 p.m., he issued his regular weather forecast. One thing in particular had caught his attention:

> A TROPICAL WAVE ... IS PRODUCING WIDESPREAD CLOUDINESS AND SCATTERED THUNDERSTORMS OVER THE CENTRAL TROPICAL ATLANTIC ABOUT 1,000 MILES EAST OF THE LEEWARD ISLANDS. THIS SYSTEM HAS A LOW CHANCE OF BECOMING A TROPICAL CYCLONE DURING THE NEXT 48 HOURS.

There was nothing unusual about this. That year's season had already seen nine hurricanes in the Atlantic basin, each of them forecast and tracked by NHC experts.

The first signs that this storm was something bigger came late on 22 October. A special **reconnaissance** aircraft, called a Hurricane Hunter, made a close study of the weather system and reported winds of 64 kilometres (40 miles) per hour. The NHC then upgraded the weather system to tropical storm status, and gave it a name: Sandy. On 24 October, Sandy was upgraded again to a full-blown hurricane.

Viewpoint from the ground

"Everybody's worried about it here, I can tell you. This storm is no small thing."

Philip Salmon, living in a **shanty town** near the US Embassy, Kingston, Jamaica

Finding shelter

NHC forecasters used **computer models** to predict that Hurricane Sandy would pass over central Jamaica, parts of Haiti and the Dominican Republic, and eastern Cuba, before hitting the Bahamas. By now, the Jamaican government had closed schools, businesses and airports. People who lived in low-lying areas likely to flood were moved into shelters on higher ground.

Jamaicans tried to prepare themselves for the hurricane. Those living in poorer parts of Kingston, Jamaica's capital, already had to cope with cracked ceilings and leaky corrugated iron roofs, often held down with rocks, even before the storm hit. In Haiti, the government did its best to warn of the coming storm and encourage people into shelters. But the majority of Haitians live in the countryside. Few had electricity, let alone phones or computers, so many people did not receive the warnings.

Weather warnings

In threatened areas, the NHC in Florida, on the east coast of the United States, issues two kinds of notices about approaching cyclones:
1. A hurricane watch shows a hurricane is possible within 48 hours.
2. A hurricane warning shows a hurricane is expected within 36 hours.

Even at this point, Sandy looked like it would pose a major threat to the US coast, too. "It's a big storm and it's going to grow in size after it leaves Cuba," said Michael Brennan, a hurricane forecaster at the NHC. The storm's **wind field** would be so big by the time it left the Bahamas that it would create "very high surf and dangerous conditions all the way up the east coast into the Carolinas".

Residents of Kingston, Jamaica, tried to protect their houses against the storm by nailing boards over windows and placing sandbags across doorways.

In the disaster zone

What was it like to face the might of Hurricane Sandy?

Jamaica

Jamaica was the first island to suffer the full force of the hurricane. Sandy's eye passed over Kingston on 24 October. Fierce winds destroyed shanty towns, and flattened trees and power lines. One man was crushed to death under a falling boulder loosened by the rain. Police imposed a **curfew** in major towns to discourage **looting** of properties abandoned by those seeking shelter elsewhere. In the capital, looters shot and wounded a police officer.

Hispaniola

Shortly afterwards, the edge of the hurricane passed over Haiti and the Dominican Republic. The clouds dumped vast amounts of rain over the next four days, causing widespread flooding and **mudslides**. More than 50 Haitians died and more than 200,000 were left homeless. The floods destroyed much of the island's crops and livestock, leading to food shortages. One farmer, Nessilo Dorestant, said, "We have lost everything. There is no possible way for my family to survive this long without food."

The people of Port-au-Prince in Haiti rescued their most valuable goods from the flood, including livestock.

Cuba

On 25 October, Sandy slashed across eastern Cuba with winds of 177 kilometres (110 miles) per hour. It killed at least 11 people and damaged over 230,000 homes. The historic city of Santiago de Cuba was worst hit. "Everything is destroyed in Santiago. People are going to have to work very hard to recover," one resident, Alexis Manduley, said.

The Morning after

"Thursday morning [26 October] will never be forgotten by thousands of people in Eastern Cuba ... that first night after the disaster in which, from their battered beds or rickety sofas, they found nothing separating their faces from the starry night sky."

Yoani Sanchez, Cuban journalist

Haiti's 2010 earthquake

In 2010, a catastrophic earthquake hit Haiti, near Port-au-Prince (the capital city and the most densely populated part of the country). Haiti is one of the world's poorest countries, and the earthquake brought widespread famine and disease. Despite foreign aid, the country is still trying to recover.

Date:	12 January 2010
Magnitude:	7.0
Casualties:	about 220,000 dead, 196,000 injured
Damage in Port-au-Prince:	190,000 houses badly damaged, 105,000 completely destroyed; 1.5 million people homeless.

A victim's point of view: homeless and hungry in Haiti

After the massive earthquake that hit Haiti in 2010 destroyed her home, Fifi Bouille was living in a huge tent city, with thousands of other homeless Haitians. When the hurricane struck, she was giving birth without any medical help. The canvas roof of her tent threatened to blow off, so she had to flee through the storm to find new shelter. "I was terrified my baby might die," she said.

"Frankenstorm" heads for the United States

On 27 October, Sandy moved away from the Caribbean and turned north-east. That night, the hurricane travelled parallel to the coastlines of Georgia, South Carolina and North Carolina. The NHC now classed it as a Category 1 hurricane, with winds of up to 128 kilometres (80 miles) per hour, although the eye of the storm stayed well off shore.

But Sandy was about to change again, from a huge storm into a monster. Jim Cisco, of the US National Weather Service, saw the spiralling hurricane was heading for a cold weather system from the Arctic. In his bulletin of 25 October, Cisco predicted the two systems would merge to create a gigantic "vortex", which would hit the United States on 29 October – close to Halloween. He gave it the nickname "Frankenstorm" (after Victor Frankenstein, creator of the monster in Mary Shelley's horror story). It became known as a "superstorm".

Close down and move out

Those people living in Sandy's path had already been preparing for the storm's arrival. Now things got urgent. US President Barack Obama signed emergency declarations for New York, Massachusetts, New Jersey and other states. This meant that schools, transport systems, shops, and factories were to close.

Many evacuees from the worst hit areas found shelter in school halls and other public buildings.

Evacuate or not: local weather forecaster's perspective

Despite warnings, many people in vulnerable areas refused to **evacuate**. Gary Szatkowski, NWS forecaster in Mount Holly, Philadelphia, put out a "personal plea" for local people to think again:

* If you are being asked to evacuate a coastal location, please do so.

* If you know someone who rode out the 1962 storm, ask them if they would do it again.

* If you are still reluctant, think about your loved ones, think about the emergency responders who will be unable to reach you when you make the panicked phone call to be rescued.

* Sandy is an extremely dangerous storm. Injuries are probably unavoidable, but the goal is zero fatalities (deaths).

* If you think the storm is over-hyped, err on the side of caution. You can call me up on Friday and yell at me all you want.

* I will tell you in advance, I will be very happy you are alive and well, no matter how much you yell at me.

On 28 October, New York City's mayor, Michael Bloomberg, ordered the evacuation of low-lying areas in the city. Over 375,000 people had to leave their homes and head for one of the emergency evacuation centres, most of which were in school buildings.

What would you do?

Imagine you are advised to seek shelter in a safer place to wait out a hurricane. Would you evacuate? Or would you stay in your home and ride out the storm? You may be risking your life. Would your actions also put other people, such as emergency workers, in danger?

Sitting tight

While thousands left their New York homes, many decided to stay put. John Miller, of Battery Park, stockpiled soup, biscuits and pasta, and filled his bath with water, in preparation for the water supply being cut off.

Kymal Raginov was one of 450 senior citizens who refused to leave their building on Coney Island. "I am scared but I hope it will pass. If anything happens, the police will save me."

New York City under water

At 12.30 p.m. on 29 October, the superstorm changed course and surged towards the US coast. The eye of the storm smashed into the New Jersey shore at 8 p.m., flooding the streets and causing widespread destruction, including felling part of the famous Atlantic City Boardwalk. At the same time, Sandy's whirling cloud system also reached New York City.

The storm's wind and rain were still ferocious. But its most astonishing feature was the wall of water it flung at the shore. Whipped up by the winds and made still taller by an exceptionally high tide, the storm surge reached nearly 4.3 metres (14 feet) above the low water mark as it roared into New York Harbor. It overflowed the sea wall in Lower Manhattan, flooding parts of the underground train system and a major road tunnel.

Surviving a superstorm

The raw power of Superstorm Sandy took many New Yorkers by surprise. As winds of 128 kilometres (80 miles) per hour roared through the city, house roofs were blown off, windows shattered and tall structures rocked. Floods filled basements and swept away vehicles and other property. Many buildings were left unsafe to live in. Power supplies were damaged, and at one time almost 2 million people throughout New York State had no electricity.

Some people were forced to climb onto their roofs to escape the rising waters. Daphay Sanchez and her husband, on Staten Island, tied themselves together so that they would not slide off their roof. They had to cling on for eight hours before they were rescued. Kim Joyce, also of Staten Island, had to swim to get away from her flooded home, carrying her two cats.

View from a shelter

The Seward Park High School in Lower Manhattan was just one of 76 hurricane shelters. As the storm raged on, 1,100 evacuees crowded into its five floors, along with eight dogs, a cat and a rabbit. They were looked after by 30 city employees and 10 volunteers. When the electricity failed and the lights went out, a portable **generator** was set up outside. Evacuees slept in rows of green camp beds and were served three meals a day. The work was "a little hectic", said centre manager, Richard Gorgoglione.

The wreck of the *Bounty*

The superstorm brought huge dangers at sea as well as on land. A major tragedy was the sinking of the *Bounty*, a replica of an 18th-century sailing ship. When the hurricane hit, the ship was halfway between Connecticut and Florida. As the ship began to sink, most of the crew of 16 boarded lifeboats and were rescued by US Coast Guard helicopters. The captain and another crew member drowned.

A crane on a half-built skyscraper in New York City was so badly battered by Sandy's winds that it dangled over the streets below.

DOSSIER:
SANDY'S IMPACT ON NORTH AMERICA

Besides causing many deaths and enormous damage on the US north-east coast, Superstorm Sandy also brought chaos to many other US states, and to Canada. The whole of the eastern seaboard, from Florida to Maine, was affected by heavy rain and storm surges. Freakishly heavy snow blizzards hit the Appalachian Mountains in West Virginia, and high winds rocked buildings and felled power lines in Ohio. Storm-force winds raced across southern Ontario, Canada.

This map of the eastern United States and Canada shows the main areas affected by the superstorm.

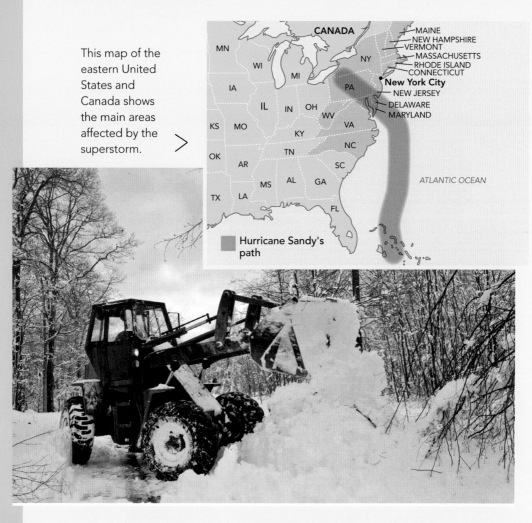

CANADA

MN
WI
MI
IA
IL   IN   OH
KS   MO
WV
KY
OK
TN
AR
MS   AL   GA
TX   LA
FL

NY
PA
VA
NC
SC

MAINE
NEW HAMPSHIRE
VERMONT
MASSACHUSETTS
RHODE ISLAND
CONNECTICUT
New York City
NEW JERSEY
DELAWARE
MARYLAND

ATLANTIC OCEAN

Hurricane Sandy's path

National Guard members cleared roads to electricity plants so that engineers could repair them and restore the supply.

QUICK FACTS

DURATION:	29 October to 1 November
NUMBER OF PEOPLE AFFECTED:	60 million
FLIGHTS CANCELLED, 27 OCT–2 NOV:	20,500
HIGHEST STORM SURGE:	4.3 m (14.5 ft.) above average low water level, at Bergen Point, New York City
HEAVIEST RAINFALL:	0.3 m (12.8 in.) in Bellevue, Maryland
HEAVIEST SNOWFALL:	0.9 m (36 in.) in Richwood, West Virginia
DEBRIS LEFT BY THE STORM IN NEW JERSEY AND NEW YORK:	8.4 million cubic metres (12 million cubic yards)
DEATHS:	72 in the US, due directly to the storm, plus 87 indirect deaths (from causes such as accidents during the clean-up, and exposure to cold weather); 1 direct death in Canada, plus 1 indirect death (from **electrocution**)
ESTIMATED COST:	$65 billion in United States; CAD$100 million in Canada

SANDY'S LAST DAYS TIMELINE

29 OCTOBER
The superstorm comes ashore on the coasts of New Jersey and New York. At one point, 8.5 million people in the affected states are without electricity.

30 OCTOBER
The hurricane weakens and moves inland from New York. It still brings mayhem to the north-east, including major blizzards of snow in the Appalachian Mountains.

31 OCTOBER
Tropical Storm Sandy begins to dissipate (fade away) over western Pennsylvania

1 NOVEMBER
The last remnants fade away across the **Great Lakes** and into Canada, bringing more rain and snow

The emergency services react

How did the aftermath of Hurricane Sandy look to emergency service workers?

Rooftop drama

The police helicopter hovered over the Staten Island street. Down below, crouched on a flat roof, one of the crew finished securing a woman in the rescue basket. Then he waved to the winch operator above, who hauled the basket slowly up to safety. The dark floodwaters stretched around the buildings, just a metre below the roofs.

On this mission of 30 October, the New York Police Department helicopter rescued six people, including a child, from the neighbourhood. They had been trapped on their roofs due to the rising waters. The officers were members of the NYPD Aviation and Scuba division, which saved scores of people from Sandy's floodwaters.

Fire in the flood

Fire is not the most obvious threat from flooding. Yet 94 separate fires broke out in New York in the wake of the storm, most of them started by electrical or gas explosions. The worst was at Breezy Point, Queens, where 126 homes were destroyed on 29 October. More than 200 firefighters were called to control the massive blaze, which raged for 45 hours. Amazingly, there were no deaths or injuries.

A rescuer's story

US *People* magazine reported that police chief Thomas Boyd took a truck with fire chief James Samarelli through rising waters on 29 October to save 36 stranded people in Seaside Heights, New Jersey:

"I said, 'Anybody who wants to leave, go. I'm staying.' Their response? 'Chief, if you're staying, we're staying'. They put their lives on the line for me. The water started filling up the truck, and I told Samarelli, 'This is not a good situation here. If the water flips us, we're dead.' We plucked one kid out of a tree. We saved a three-year-old, a seven-year-old, and a pregnant mother up in an attic. If we didn't rescue them, they would not be here today."

Search and rescue

Rescue workers also moved stranded New Yorkers by boat – and some even waded through the waters, carrying storm victims in their arms. Units from the US National Guard and the Marine Corps, along with other relief workers, checked on those who had not been evacuated. Specially trained dog teams searched wrecked buildings to sniff out humans (and pets) who were trapped or alone. Some of those who decided not to evacuate did not survive.

Managing the response

The **Federal Emergency Management Agency (FEMA)** also responded to the disaster. FEMA's co-ordinating officer in New York during the disaster was Michael Byrne. He said, "I knew our response was going to have to be huge. I knew that in a city of 8 million, we were not going to have enough boots on the ground. Luckily, FEMA had planned for that need." Within 48 hours of Sandy's landfall, they had 1,200 people in the field, going door to door in affected neighbourhoods of New York City.

Helicopter crews rescued many people stranded and in danger during the hurricane. These Coast Guards hoisted 14 survivors from a sinking ship off North Carolina.

21

Medical aid in the United States

Besides the many dead, there were countless people left injured or ill and in need of immediate treatment. But even the US's modern health service struggled to cope with the aftermath of the storm. More than 2,300 emergency staff were drafted into hospitals and medical centres in New York, as well as 350 additional ambulances from other areas. Some operated mobile vans, providing care and prescription drugs in places where normal medical centres were out of action.

The floods also knocked out electricity supplies over much of the city. This was a massive threat to safety in hospitals, where power was vital for surgical operations and many other procedures. At the height of the storm, even the emergency electricity generators at New York University Hospital broke down. More than 200 patients had to be evacuated, including very ill newborn babies, who needed **respirators** to breathe. With no power to run the respirators, nurses carried each baby down nine flights of stairs, squeezing a bag by hand to push air into each baby's lungs.

Medical aid in Haiti

The United States is a large and wealthy country, with a vast network of disaster agencies. But in the Caribbean, things are very different. The countries hit by the storm were small and some, such as Haiti, were very poor, with few emergency resources. Haiti was also still struggling from the effects of previous natural disasters. The country depended largely on foreign aid and donations from charitable organizations.

The biggest medical problem lay in the tent camps near Port-au-Prince, where over 320,000 homeless people had lived since the 2010 earthquake. Here, there had been a long-standing **epidemic** of **cholera**, which had killed 7,500 Haitians. Cholera is a waterborne disease, and Sandy's floods had spread it rapidly. The government reported eight new cholera deaths a week after the hurricane. The Red Cross and other medical charities began giving out hygiene kits and water purification tablets in an attempt to combat the epidemic.

Rescue workers need health care, too

When most people are trying to leave disaster zones, emergency service workers and volunteers are entering these often dangerous places. They face broken power lines, collapsed buildings and exposure to **contaminated** water and **toxic** chemicals. Workers are trained to deal with the **traumatic** conditions, but it is a harsh environment to work in. Some had to recover dead bodies or deal with the extreme distress of **bereaved** or injured people.

However, a large number of rescue workers had no free health benefits. For instance, 70 per cent of FEMA's workforce did not receive federal (official government) health insurance. This meant they had to pay for their own health care. After the hurricane, charity worker Dena Patrick started an online petition to change this. "I feel that our priorities are skewed," she said. Her petition went **viral**, and by 13 November the government had agreed to give free health care to first responders.

Ambulances lined up outside Bellevue Hospital in New York City to evacuate 500 patients after floodwater caused the electricity supply to fail.

Shelter and food

Many disaster survivors had lost homes and belongings. Their first need was shelter. But, without transport, and with most food shops shut or hit by the storm, victims were also in desperate need of food and clean drinking water. In New York, distribution sites were set up to distribute food, bottled water and blankets. The US National Guard carried supplies to old or ill people in high-rise blocks.

The US government provided money for home repairs in the form of federal disaster assistance. By 2 November, more than 36,000 superstorm victims from New York, New Jersey and Connecticut had applied for money, and more than $3.4 million had been promised in individual grants. As well as home repair, this money could be used for rent for temporary housing and loans to cover damaged properties that were not insured.

Free fuel fiasco

Supplies of petrol ran low in New York after the storm, leaving most people unable to use their vehicles. On 3 November, Governor Andrew Cuomo announced the city would be giving out free fuel for both "emergency vehicles and the general public". The result was chaos, as hundreds of motorists jammed the roads, waiting to fill up. Cuomo was later forced to withdraw the offer.

A rescuer's story

"Haitian authorities were able to evacuate vulnerable people – like the disabled and women with small children ... For everyone else, there is simply nowhere to go and the camps and tents are completely flooded. Latrines [toilets] have overflowed and garbage is everywhere. Tomorrow we are going to start distributing emergency kits that include plastic sheeting, jerry cans for collecting water, wind-up flashlights [torches], hygiene supplies and other items ..."

Miriam Castaneda, leader of the International Rescue Committee's humanitarian aid programmes in Haiti

Problems in the shelters

For all its resources, the US relief effort ran into major difficulties. Soon after the storm, over 7,000 people took refuge in New York's emergency evacuation shelters. Most of these had lost their homes in the hurricane, due to flooding or wind damage. These places kept the evacuees safe during the worst of the hurricane, but in the following days major problems began to appear. Public shelters, where men, women and children were crowded together, were not safe or suitable over a long period of time.

Crime and disease were the biggest hazards, and some shelters quickly became filthy and dangerous. Journalist Lindsey Christ was shocked by one school on West 49th Street. She wrote, "It smelled like a sewer. Some classrooms are labeled 'for families', but there were no security checks. Many of the bathrooms were out of order. Clothing was flushed down toilets. We saw empty alcohol bottles."

US Naval helicopters ferried emergency supplies from ships at sea to the people of Haiti after Hurricane Sandy.

DOSSIER:
HOW TO SURVIVE A HURRICANE

A hurricane poses many life-threatening dangers. At sea, high winds and **rip currents** can sink ships. Storm surges bring floods to coastal areas, but heavy rains may be even more dangerous. They dump water further inland, causing lethal flooding far from the coast. Records show that, since the 1980s, more people have died in inland floods than in storm surges. Rain also causes mudslides and **erosion**. Hurricane-force winds damage buildings and fell trees, turning debris into deadly missiles. What are the best ways to survive such a catastrophic event?

QUICK FACTS

The safest thing to do is to evacuate. If you cannot, here is FEMA's list of basic disaster supplies:

- Water (3.8 litres/8 pints per person a day, for three days)
- Food (**non-perishable**, enough for three days)
- Battery-powered or **wind-up radio**
- Weather radio (plus extra batteries)
- Torch (plus extra batteries)
- First aid kit
- Whistle (to signal for help)
- Dust mask (to filter contaminated air)
- Plastic sheeting and **duct tape** (to make a shelter)
- Wet wipes, bin bags and plastic ties (for personal sanitation)
- Wrench or pliers (to turn off utilities)
- Manual can opener
- Local maps
- Mobile phone with charger

∧ Supermarket shelves emptied fast as people stocked up with food and other supplies before the storm hit.

Case studies

Don't give up trying

Mike lived on the New Jersey coast. When he walked out of his front door on the night of the hurricane, floodwaters picked him up and swept him 800 metres out into Silver Bay. He reckons he was in the water for four or five hours, trying to swim against the swirling currents. At last he made it back ashore some way down the coast, half-drowned and suffering from **hypothermia**. All the houses there were empty, so he broke into one and found a blanket and some water. He was eventually rescued.

Take shelter wherever you can

As Sandy approached, Jeremy Goodman, then working at New Jersey's Turtle Back Zoo, set about protecting his 700 animals. One by one, staff moved them into a safe building and stocked up on vital supplies. They also took in 25 people from a nearby shelter. Parents and their children spent the night with pythons, poisonous tree frogs, a Komodo dragon, a wolf and many other creatures – many of them dangerous. All survived.

Keep your nerve

At the height of the storm, a team of New York firefighters were tackling a blaze. They spotted 16 people, including children, clinging to a roof. Flames roared over their heads, while floodwater rose beneath them. "They were either going to burn to death or drown," said team commander Lieutenant Bob LaRocco. The firefighters took a boat to the burning building, mooring it to an electricity pole. If this had fallen, they would have been electrocuted. They climbed to the roof and helped the people down. The boat was now full, so the rescuers had to stay outside it and wade back to safety. All survived.

Telling the world

Before Sandy had hit land, the media had been reporting on the storm. Now, as the story changed from minute to minute, it became **rolling news**, with non-stop coverage and regular updates.

Taking risks

Journalists, camera operators and photographers often had to record or broadcast live reports from dramatic settings in the hurricane. This often put them in danger.

- ABC reporter Matt Gutman and his producer were preparing to film a piece on Nags Head beach, North Carolina, USA, as the storm hit. A rogue wave knocked the pair over and they had to scramble to shore.

- Ali Velshi, who at that time worked for CNN, reported in the high winds and rain in Atlantic City, New Jersey, USA. Some locals, including the city's mayor, Lorenzo Langford, criticized him for ignoring warnings to stay inside, safe from the danger. But Velshi told his viewers that his team knew the dangers and had taken precautions. He said, "We've done this before, and we know how to keep safe."

BREAKING NEWS
EYE OF STORM HITS GALVESTON WITH 110-MILE-AN-HOUR W
A METROLINK COMM

Many television news reporters braved high winds, waves and lashing rain to show how bad conditions were.

Social media

Like many recent big events, ordinary people told the story of Hurricane Sandy through social media such as Twitter, Facebook and YouTube. With instant streaming, sharing and personal views generated by those sitting in the eye of the storm, this was the first port of call for information about the hurricane for many millions of people all over the world. Journalists also made use of these resources, trawling them for information, and speaking to online communities to confirm facts. Online journalist Markham Nolan said, "the volume [of social media stories] was incredible. We'd never seen anything like that before."

Superstorm chasers

Unlike **tornadoes**, which can appear suddenly, hurricanes are easy to find and follow because they are gigantic and move at about the speed of a road vehicle. People who follow them are called storm chasers. Most chasers are professionals. They enter storms with special monitoring equipment to gather important data, such as **humidity**, air pressure, temperature and wind speeds.

But some are also there for the thrill of experiencing a violent natural event. They take videos and photographs, and put the footage on social media websites. Their footage is often broadcast on television.

Hunting tools

The aircraft used by the Hurricane Hunter unit are fitted with state-of-the-art devices for collecting storm data.

- "Weatherbird" computer software: This monitors atmospheric conditions near the aircraft and automatically relays the figures to the NHC.
- A **dropsonde**: This is a lightweight pack of instruments that is dropped out of the aircraft. As it falls, slowed by a parachute, it measures air pressure, temperature, and wind speed and direction.
- The Vertical Profiling System: This on-board system receives the data from the dropsonde and processes it to give a picture of weather conditions below the aircraft – all the way to the ocean.

Flying into the storm

The most famous professional storm chasers are the Hurricane Hunters, a unit of US Air Force reservists (some of whom work part-time) who take specially equipped aircraft near and even into hurricanes and other big storms to report back to the NHC. The unit may fly up to three missions a day in the cyclone season. From its main base at Biloxi, Mississippi, the unit covers a vast area, from the mid-Pacific to the Caribbean and the mid-Atlantic.

Through the eye

What is it like to take an aircraft right through the eye of a tropical storm? Jon Talbot, a Hurricane Hunter, flew through Sandy twice:

"We fly at [3,000 kilometres] 10,000 feet, and the idea is to go right through the centre of the hurricane so you can measure the core of the storm, and then also measure the winds on the **periphery** of the storm. It normally gets very rough right near the centre, and then out away from the centre when the winds lighten up, it's not so bad anymore."

Talbot claims that while sometimes flying through a tropical storm can be "nasty", Sandy was "relatively uneventful".

Why do they do it? The answer is simple: flying is the only way to get accurate and wide-ranging information about storm systems over the sea. Data collected by the Hurricane Hunters allows **meteorologists** to make precise forecasts about how a hurricane will move and behave. This gives people on the ground plenty of warning about exactly where the storm might strike, and saves lives and money. During the build-up of Hurricane Sandy, Hurricane Hunter aircraft flew many missions into the weather system, tracking its size, direction and changing wind strength.

In this picture, you can just see the tip of the wing of the aircraft from where the photo was taken.

The Bhola Cyclone of November 1970 flooded much of Bangladesh (then called East Pakistan). It was probably the deadliest of all modern natural disasters, killing as many as 1 million people. This region is especially vulnerable to flooding, because it is low-lying and has major rivers running through it. It is also very densely populated, because of its fertile farmland. The storm surge from the cyclone flooded islands and coastal areas, wiping out many communities.

Creating a new nation

The Bhola Cyclone also changed the political world map. The people of East Pakistan were angry with their local government for failing to respond quickly to the catastrophe, and elected an opposition group to power. The unrest grew, and it eventually led to a war, which resulted in independence from Pakistan. In 1971, the new state of Bangladesh was created.

This map shows the track of the Bhola Cyclone northwards from the Indian Ocean to the Bay of Bengal.

>

The storm surge pushed floodwater over vast areas of East Pakistan.

∨

INDIA

Ganges

Brahmaputra

EAST PAKISTAN
(now Bangladesh)

Dhaka

Chittagong

BURMA

Bay of Bengal

Indian
Ocean

Bhola Cyclone
path

DATES:	8–13 November 1970
HIGHEST SUSTAINED WIND SPEEDS:	185 km (115 mi.) per hour: there were also gusts measured at 225 km (140 mi.) per hour
STORM SURGE HEIGHT:	10 m (32 ft.)
AFFECTED AREA:	6,000 sq. km (2,300 sq. mi.)
DEATHS:	official toll 300,000–500,000, but probably nearer 1 million
HOMELESS:	2.5 million
COST:	$86.4 million (at 1970 values – equivalent of $508 million today)

THE BHOLA CYCLONE TIMELINE

The Bhola Cyclone was never measured with accurate meteorological instruments, so it is not possible to reconstruct the whole story precisely. Here is what experts believe happened.

8 NOVEMBER
A depression (area of low pressure) forms in the Bay of Bengal

9 NOVEMBER
Bhola strengthens into a tropical storm

11 NOVEMBER
The winds increase to cyclone speeds and head north-east

12 NOVEMBER
The Bhola Cyclone makes landfall on the coast of East Pakistan

13 NOVEMBER
The cyclone dissipates over southern Assam

Scientists at work

Hurricane Sandy was terrifying for the people living in its path. But for scientists, it was an exciting opportunity. By monitoring the superstorm, they could discover more about how these freak weather systems behaved. This in turn would help them to forecast the arrival and impact of future storms.

Studying Sandy

The tropical depression which was to become Hurricane Sandy first appeared in the middle of the Atlantic on 19 October. It was detected on a computer screen over 1,600 kilometres away, at the National Hurricane Center (NHC) in Miami, Florida.

The experts' job was to monitor weather systems in the Atlantic and eastern Pacific, and predict how they would develop. For this, they used data from many sources, including:

- weather satellites orbiting Earth
- observation stations in the south-east United States, Caribbean, Central America and West Africa
- **radar** stations across the United States.

The development of storm systems in the Atlantic is followed closely on computer monitors at the National Hurricane Center.

Saffir-Simpson Hurricane Wind Scale
This scale, which is named after the scientists who created it, grades five scales of hurricane.

Category	Wind speed	Types of damage
1	119–153 km (74–95 mi.) per hour	Very dangerous winds will produce some damage
2	154–177 km (96–110 mi.) per hour	Extremely dangerous winds will cause extensive damage
3	178–208 km (111–129 mi.) per hour	Devastating damage will occur: houses will be damaged and trees will be snapped or uprooted
4	209–251 km (130–156 mi.) per hour	Catastrophic damage will occur: houses will be severely damaged. Most of the area will be uninhabitable for weeks or months.
5	252 km (157 mi.) or higher per hour	Catastrophic damage: a high percentage of houses will be destroyed, with collapsed roofs and walls

Where will it hit?

By collecting and analysing information about air pressure, wind speeds, sea surface temperatures and many other factors, the scientists were able to track Sandy as it grew from a depression into a superstorm. The Hurricane Specialist Unit staff then put their findings through computer modelling programs. In this way they were able to predict the superstorm's track with amazing accuracy.

On 24 October, five days before the storm made landfall, they pinpointed the place where it would come ashore – and were only 48 kilometres (30 miles) out. This was a huge improvement on previous hurricane forecasts, which had sometimes been over 480 kilometres (300 miles) out. "If Hurricane Sandy happened 20 years back, it would almost certainly have been a disaster without much warning," said meteorologist Sundararaman Gopalakrishnan.

After the storm

In preparation for the hurricane season, **US Geological Survey (USGS)** scientists had installed hundreds of measuring instruments along the eastern US coastline. Then, as soon as it was safe, more than 160 USGS technicians retrieved the instruments and studied the information they had logged.

Tidal and storm-surge sensors showed record heights in many places. Crews also monitored high-water marks along the shoreline, and sampled the quality of river water near the sea to check for pollution. Meanwhile, USGS aircraft recorded how the massive waves had changed the coastline.

The future of forecasting

What is the most likely way to die in a hurricane? The answer is: drowning. Figures show that floods kill more people than any other hurricane hazard. More than a third of all of Superstorm Sandy's victims drowned because of the flooding from the record-breaking surge.

Even before Sandy appeared in 2012, scientists at the International Hurricane Research Center (IHRC) in Florida had been developing a new way of predicting storm surges and how they would behave. Aircraft using an advanced radar system called Light Detection and Ranging (LIDAR) produced new maps of the Florida coast. These maps were far more accurate and detailed than any created before. For instance, LIDAR took vertical readings every 15 centimetres (6 inches). On the old maps, readings were every 1.15 metres (60 inches). That is "literally the difference between getting your feet wet and drowning", as the researchers pointed out.

With this mass of precise data, the IHRC scientists developed computer models of the coastline, with all its complex shapes and features. Combining these with details of tides and winds, they were able to forecast exactly how a storm surge would affect the region when it hit. The resulting information was passed on to emergency managers and services.

How accurate can hurricane forecasts be?

Nature will never be totally predictable, even with the most advanced computer modelling. Even so, staff at the NHC have been forecasting the behaviour of tropical storms more and more accurately. Since 1990, they have reduced errors by 60 per cent. New systems also allow them to make firm forecasts five days ahead, instead of three days ahead as it was previously.

Reaching the limit

"Everyone wants us to do more and more and more ... and sometimes the best answer is to say, 'No, we're not capable of meeting that need.'"

James Franklin, Chief of NHC's Hurricane Specialist Unit

Learning from experience

"Superstorm Sandy brought home some valuable lessons to emergency managers across the state. Storm surge and flooding are dangerous and difficult to predict, and sometimes it's even harder to communicate that sense of urgency to the public."

Rick Knabb, NHC Director

When was Sandy a hurricane?

As Sandy approached the east coast of the United States on 27 October, the NHC refused to issue a hurricane warning for the area north of North Carolina. This was because scientists expected the superstorm to weaken just before it hit land, so it would not technically be a hurricane beyond that point. But many meteorologists criticized the NHC for this. They believed it would confuse people, who might underestimate the storm's power and not take correct precautions. The NHC later altered its policy on hurricane warnings.

Researchers at the Florida International University's engineering centre have built a huge "Wall of Wind". Its twelve huge fans can generate wind speeds of over 240 kilometres (150 miles) per hour, to simulate the force of a hurricane.

Climate change and hurricanes

Superstorm Sandy was a huge natural disaster. Very few hurricanes have caused such widespread devastation. Sandy made a sharp turn to the left before smashing into the east coast of the United States. This was very unusual. Timothy Hall, of the National Aeronautics and Space Administration (NASA), suggests a storm like this might happen only once every 700 years.

However, Hall also gave a warning: we should not relax and assume there will not be a similar surge for another 700 years. Experts now agree that our climate is changing rapidly. The burning of fossil fuels and other activities have caused the atmosphere to get warmer. Many scientists believe global warming is increasing the number and intensity of cyclones across the world.

Higher surges a certainty

"The thing I am quite sure about is sea-level rise. That will continue to add to storm surges like this."

Michael Oppenheimer, US climate scientist who contributed to research on New York City's future flood surges

Climate changes facts and figures

A report on the state of the world's climate by the US National Oceanic and Atmospheric Administration showed that 2012 broke a lot of records:

- The level of man-made **greenhouse gases** in the atmosphere reached 392 parts per million for the first time.
- There was record ice loss from melting glaciers.
- Sea levels rose 3 centimetres (1.4 inches) on average.
- The amount of heat stored in the oceans reached a new high.
- The extent of Arctic sea ice reached a new low.

Will hurricanes get worse?

NASA and other agencies are now researching the ways in which climate change is influencing the weather. Many theories have already been put forward:

- More powerful storms: Global warming has heated the oceans and the air to higher temperatures. This creates more water vapour and rain, producing ideal conditions for cyclones to grow bigger than ever.

- More frequent storms: The heating of the oceans also means major cyclones are likely to occur more often in the North Pacific, the North Atlantic and the south Indian Ocean.

- Bigger storm surges: The hotter climate is melting the polar ice caps, which in turn is raising the level of the seas. This will make storm surges higher, bringing an even greater threat to low-lying coastal regions.

- Less predictable hurricane tracks: Warmer air at the North Pole may weaken the force of the **jet stream**, which usually blows hurricanes out into the Atlantic. Without this, the storm systems could move towards land more frequently.

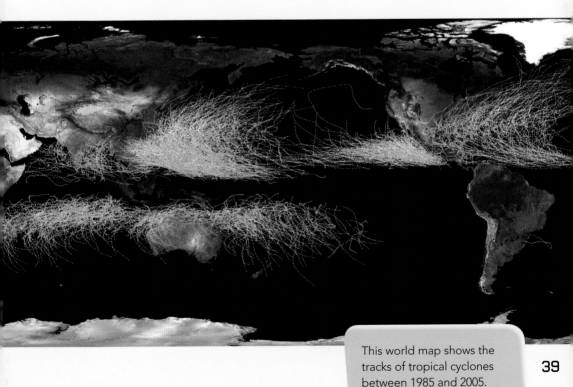

This world map shows the tracks of tropical cyclones between 1985 and 2005.

39

DOSSIER:
HURRICANE KATRINA

Hurricane Katrina, which struck the southern United States in August 2005, was one of the worst natural disasters ever to hit the country. It had much stronger winds and was more costly and deadly than Sandy, causing the deaths of more than 1,800 people. The greatest loss of life occurred in New Orleans, Louisiana, which the storm reached on 29 August. The final death toll for the city of New Orleans alone was over 1,400. Then-US President George W. Bush and state officials were later criticized for bad planning and a slow response to the emergency.

This map shows the path of Hurricane Katrina across the Caribbean and into the Gulf of Mexico.

>

Katrina's storm surge caused several disastrous breaches (breaks) in the levees that were built to protect New Orleans from flooding.

∨

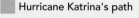
Hurricane Katrina's path

HURRICANE KATRINA TIMELINE

23 AUGUST
The NHC reports a tropical depression over the Bahamas

25 AUGUST
Katrina strengthens to hurricane force and comes ashore near Miami, Florida

27 AUGUST
Katrina strengthens to a Category 3 hurricane

28 AUGUST
Katrina, now Category 5, heads for the Louisiana coast

29 AUGUST
The storm comes ashore again. Many levees fail in New Orleans.

30 AUGUST
Katrina dissipates over Tennessee

Breaching the levees

The New Orleans tragedy was mainly due to an engineering failure. The city is very low-lying, much of it below the level of the Mississippi River on one side and Lake Pontchartrain on the other. From 1985, the **levees**, which kept the water back, had been extended and strengthened by the US Army Corps of Engineers. However, there were 28 breaches on the day of the storm, and many more later. The Corps of Engineers later admitted the levee designs were faulty.

Recovery and reconstruction

Twelve mountains of sand stood in Jacob Riis Park, New York City, each as tall as a house. It was January 2013, less than three months after Hurricane Sandy. The sand had been hurled across the coastal areas by the storm, but in the following weeks it had been swept up, carried across town and cleaned. Each truckload of sand was passed through giant screens, which sifted out the debris. This too was piled up, ready to be taken away.

The debris included bricks, post boxes, shoes, clothing, telephone poles, shop signs and all sorts of rubbish. "A lot of people's lives are out on the [pavement] here," said George Kroenert, an official helping with the clean-up. Over 10,800 lorryloads of debris were hauled out of the city and buried in landfill sites. The cleaned sand was to be returned to the beaches.

Some of the thousands of vehicles damaged by the floods were retrieved and stored on Calverton Airpark, just outside New York City.

After the event

In the United States, some people were able to move back home soon after the storm. But thousands more had a long wait. Even by April 2013, over 39,000 inhabitants of New Jersey were still homeless.

- Jennifer Burke lost her home in a fire. Rebuilding had not yet started. She said, "We're just still waiting and still hoping. The hardest part is just not knowing."
- Barry Fischer had just moved back into his repaired house with a wife and five children. "The three greatest words in the English language: home sweet home," he said.
- Ginjer Doherty was only nine years old when Sandy struck. She said, "My house was all messed up, and people told us we couldn't stay there anymore". But even after six months, repairs had not begun.

The long road to recovery

Here are some of the other urgent operations being tackled by armies of state and city workers, contractors, military staff and volunteers:

- Pumping out water: New York's Metropolitan Transportation Authority sent giant "pump trains" underground to suck out floodwaters from underground tunnels. The three pumps on the trains each sent 5,678 litres (1,500 gallons) of water back into the Hudson River every minute. "Everyone is working around the clock," said Tommy Dropp, a pump-train operator. "Workers. Management. Nobody's standing around. We want to get this water down. We want to get it off the track."

- Restoring electricity supplies: A fortnight after the storm, power companies were still working flat out to return power to 8.5 million people. On Long Island alone, about 6,400 linemen and 3,700 **tree trimmers** were at work, compared with 200 on a normal day. Some New Yorkers did not get power restored until December.

- Demolishing damaged homes: In New York City, at least 200 houses were so badly damaged by the storm and floods that they had to be torn down. Another 200 had already been wrecked. In New Jersey, the total was much higher: 46,000. The rubble from all these ruins was bulldozed and cleared away.

Helping after the hurricane

Even a wealthy, well-organized country like the United States found it hard to cope with the devastating legacy of Hurricane Sandy. For a poor country like Haiti, the struggle to recover was much more difficult. The storm caused $600 million worth of damage to buildings, roads, bridges and water supply systems. It destroyed 150 schools. Most crops were also wiped out, meaning that up to 2 million Haitians faced long-term food shortages.

Help was desperately needed – not just from foreign governments, but from emergency charities and international organizations such as the United Nations. But since the 2010 earthquake, Haiti had received huge amounts of foreign aid. Hundreds of aid workers were already in place in camps and other local communities. Now the job had just got a lot bigger.

Haitian relief staff worked round the clock to unload and distribute food and fresh water to people made homeless by Superstorm Sandy.

The cost of natural disasters

How much do natural disasters cost the world every year, both in human and monetary terms? Here are some recent statistics:

Year	Economic cost of disasters	Number of people affected
2010	$218 billion	207 million
2011	$371 billion	205 million
2012	$138 billion	6 million

The Red Cross

Since 2010, the American Red Cross charity has spent over $44 million to reduce the risks from disasters in Haiti, so it was well prepared for the superstorm. Before Sandy arrived, Red Cross teams and community groups visited every tent, making sure everyone knew of the danger. They also noted anyone who might need special help, such as the elderly or disabled. Straight after the storm, teams went out again to distribute food, water, plastic sheets and other emergency supplies, and to see how bad the damage was.

In several camps, the Red Cross built new drainage channels to direct floodwater away from the tents. They also helped to strengthen existing embankments and hills to give further protection against the dangers of flooding and landslides. The charity aims to work closely with residents and discover what they really need. Magalie Cesar, a Haitian community leader, said, "The American Red Cross has a better idea of this community now because it's taking its time to know us."

Concerts for hope and relief

After the 2010 earthquake, an all-star charity concert was organized to raise money for the victims. Called Hope for Haiti Now, it broadcast live on 22 January 2010 from Los Angeles, New York, London and Haiti. The two-hour concert reached an estimated 640 million viewers and raised over $61 million. Among those taking part were George Clooney, Halle Berry, Mary J. Blige and Stevie Wonder. An even bigger live concert was staged to raise money after Hurricane Sandy, on 12 December 2012 – 12:12:12: The Concert for Sandy Relief raised $35 million from ticket sales alone. All funds went to victims in the United States.

DOSSIER:
HURRICANE MITCH

Hurricane Mitch was one of the most destructive Atlantic cyclones on record. Forming in the Caribbean in October 1998, it came ashore over Central America, crossing Honduras, Guatemala and Nicaragua. Because Mitch moved slowly, it dropped vast amounts of rain on these countries, causing catastrophic flooding and mudslides.

The floods in Honduras were the worst the country experienced in the 20th century. More than 7,000 people died, and entire villages were washed away. At least half of all farm crops were wiped out. Roads, bridges, buildings, healthcare facilities, and water and sewage systems were damaged or destroyed. This had a long-lasting effect in poorer regions, because it meant many people had no homes, and could not grow food or earn money.

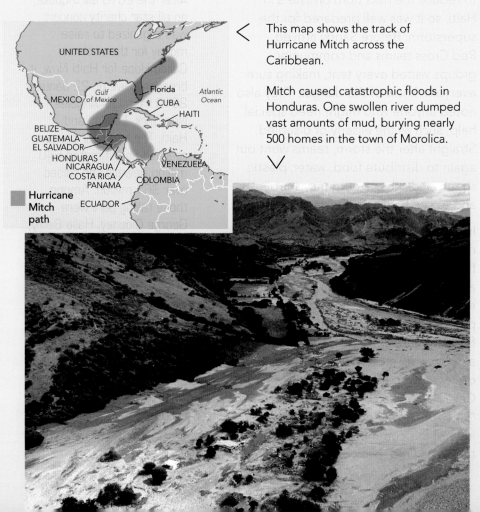

This map shows the track of Hurricane Mitch across the Caribbean.

Mitch caused catastrophic floods in Honduras. One swollen river dumped vast amounts of mud, burying nearly 500 homes in the town of Morolica.

DATES:	22 October to 5 November 1998
HIGHEST SUSTAINED WIND SPEED:	285 km (180mi.) per hour
BIGGEST RAINFALL:	0.9 m (35 in.) over Choluteca, Honduras
TOTAL RAINFALL:	1.9 m (75 in.)
CASUALTIES:	approx. 11,000; 2.7 million homeless
ESTIMATED COST:	$5 billion (at 1998 values)

Foreign aid

Immediately after the hurricane, the US government gave $80 million to affected countries in Central America. The World Bank committed over $400 million. In all, aid from around the world totalled well over $1 billion.

HURRICANE MITCH TIMELINE

21 OCTOBER
Hurricane Hunter aircraft spots a tropical depression in the southern Caribbean

22 OCTOBER
The depression strengthens into Tropical Storm Mitch

24 OCTOBER
Mitch moves westwards and strengthens to hurricane force

29–31 OCTOBER
The eye of the hurricane comes ashore over Honduras. It moves slowly over the country, dropping torrential rain.

1 NOVEMBER
Part of the storm dissipates over Guatemala and Mexico

4 NOVEMBER
The remnants of Mitch strengthen again to a tropical storm over the Caribbean

5 NOVEMBER
The storm hits the coast of Florida, USA

What have we learned?

"It should not be normal that every time it rains, we have a catastrophe throughout the country", said Haiti's Prime Minister, Laurent Lamothe, in October 2012. He was in a helicopter looking down at the swollen rivers, flooded land and shattered roads left by Hurricane Sandy. But is there anything we can do to prevent such terrible and destructive disasters?

Obviously, humans cannot stop hurricanes from forming. However, there must be ways of improving how we prepare for them, and how we cope with them when they happen. Here are some suggestions:

- Building better flood defences: Some regions (especially on the US eastern seaboard) have special walls and drainage systems to hold back the worst effects of storm surges and torrential rains. These could be made bigger and stronger. They should also be built more widely in poorer countries such as Haiti and Honduras.

- Making storm forecasting more accurate and dependable: As we have seen on page 36, forecasting agencies such as the US National Hurricane Center, are always developing faster and more precise ways of forecasting severe storms. At the heart of this is new technology for monitoring weather systems and creating computer models of hurricane behaviour.

Hurricane Sandy left a trail of devastation across much of New Jersey and New York state.

TIMELINE:
THE RECORD HOLDERS

1899
The highest storm surge: Tropical Cyclone Mahina created a surge at least 13 m (42 ft.) high when it struck Bathurst Bay, Australia

1926
The most costly cyclone: The damage caused by the Great Miami Hurricane would, at today's values, have cost more than $140 billion

1970
The deadliest cyclone: The Bhola Cyclone, which struck Bangladesh, killed at least 300,000 people, and probably nearer 1 million

1979
The biggest cyclone: Typhoon Tip in the north-west Pacific had gale-force winds that stretched for 1,100 km (675 mi.) from its centre

1996
The fastest winds: Tropical Cyclone Olivia, which struck Australia, recorded a maximum sustained wind speed of 407 km (253 mi.) per hour

2008
The smallest cyclone: Tropical Storm Marco had gale-force winds that only extended 19 km (12 mi.) from its centre

- Constructing fewer houses on low-lying ground: With rising oceans, many coastal areas are now much more vulnerable to storm surges. Ideally, all new housing developments should be constructed on higher ground, away from potential flooding. Of course, existing city homes cannot all be rebuilt. But can they be adapted to make them safer – for example by putting all living spaces at least one storey above ground level?

- Evacuating people in vulnerable areas more quickly: During Hurricane Sandy, some critics believed Mayor Bloomberg was too slow to order the evacuation of threatened areas of New York. This led, they said, to unnecessary danger and even deaths. Should the areas have been evacuated much earlier? Hundreds of people also refused to abandon their homes. Should they have been legally forced to move out?

Can you come up with any more ways of cutting down on loss of life and damage created by superstorms?

Timeline

11 October
A tropical wave (area of low pressure) starts moving across the Atlantic from West Africa

19 October
The wave reaches the central Atlantic, monitored by the National Hurricane Center in Florida, USA

22 October
The wave, now a tropical depression (with even lower air pressure), moves into the south-western Caribbean Sea and grows into a tropical storm, codenamed Sandy

24 October
Sandy strengthens into a Category 1 hurricane and moves north, causing massive damage in Jamaica, and floods in Haiti and the Dominican Republic

25 October
Now a Category 2 hurricane, Sandy crosses eastern Cuba, killing 11 people and destroying 15,000 homes

26 October
The hurricane tracks across the Bahamas, bringing more devastation. New York governor Andrew Cuomo declares a statewide emergency.

27 October
Sandy briefly weakens to a tropical storm before strengthening again to Category 1. It turns north towards the US coast.

28 October
The hurricane meets a cold weather system, which creates more energy and begins the change into a superstorm. US President Barack Obama declares emergencies in several states, including Pennsylvania, Connecticut, New York and New Jersey.

29 October
Sandy makes landfall in the United States, striking New Jersey and New York, where its huge storm surge causes major flooding

30 October	The hurricane weakens and moves inland from New York, bringing major blizzards to the Appalachian Mountains
31 October	Tropical Storm Sandy begins to dissipate over western Pennsylvania. Over 16 million people in the eastern United States are still without electricity.
1 November	The last remnants fade away across the Great Lakes and into Canada, bringing more rain and snow
7 November	Most schools in New York City re-open after the storm
8 November	Fuel rationing is imposed on New York's motorists
12 December	12:12:12: The Concert for Sandy takes place in New York to raise money for victims

Glossary

atmosphere envelope of gases that surrounds Earth

bereaved suffering distress after the death of someone or something

cholera highly infectious and deadly waterborne disease

computer model way of creating a moving image of an actual object or process on a computer

contaminated made impure or poisonous

curfew regulation requiring people to remain indoors, often at nighttime

cyclone tropical storm system with winds at high speed

dense when the parts of something, for example molecules, are crowded together

depression region of low air pressure

dropsonde radio monitoring equipment dropped by parachute

duct tape strong, often waterproof sticky tape

electrocution death by electric shock

epidemic outbreak of disease that spreads widely and rapidly

equator imaginary line drawn around the middle of Earth, dividing it into the northern and southern hemispheres

erosion process during which water or wind wears away rock or soil

evacuate move people away from a threatened area

Federal Emergency Management Agency (FEMA) US government agency that helps people before and after disasters

flash flood sudden rush of water, often destructive to anything in its path, caused by heavy rainfall

generator machine that converts mechanical energy into electrical energy

Great Lakes group of five massive freshwater lakes between Canada and the United States

greenhouse gases gases in the atmosphere (notably carbon dioxide and methane) that absorb heat from the sun, causing an increase in the warming of Earth

humidity amount of water vapour in the air

hurricane basin one of the main regions of the world where cyclones are formed

hydrogen bomb (also known as "nuclear bomb") explosive weapon that uses the energy from both splitting and fusing (joining up) atoms

hypothermia dangerously low body temperature caused by exposure to cold weather or water

jet stream narrow band of very strong, usually westerly air currents that circle Earth

levee embankment built to stop a river overflowing

loot steal from a damaged or empty property

meteorologist scientist who studies the weather

molecule very tiny particle that makes up all matter

mudslide landslide of mud caused when heavy rain falls on soil in mountainous areas

National Guard volunteer soldiers who serve each US state in times of emergency and war

non-perishable foods that do not spoil or decay, such as tinned or dried foods

periphery outside edge of something

radar system of detecting distant objects by bouncing radio waves off them

reconnaissance visiting or exploring an area to gather information about it

respirator machine that pumps air into someone's lungs when they are having trouble breathing

rip current area in the sea where two strong currents meet each other, causing dangerous conditions

rolling news round-the-clock reporting of news events

shanty town area of poor-quality housing, often badly built and inhabited by people living in poverty

storm surge wall of water built up by the high winds of a cyclone or other storm

superstorm very severe tropical cyclone, hurricane or typhoon

tornadoes rapidly spinning funnel of air that stretches from the bottom of a thunderstorm to the ground, and is dangerous to those in its path

toxic poisonous or harmful to life

traumatic when something upsetting has a deep and lasting impact on someone's life

tree trimmer someone who trims trees to prevent them causing a problem for passing trains or other vehicles

tropics hot areas of the world immediately to the north (the Tropic of Cancer) and to the south (the Tropic of Capricorn) of the equator

typhoon name given to a tropical cyclone in the Western Pacific and China Sea

US Geological Survey (USGS) organization in the United States that provides advice and information about earth sciences

viral to do with the internet, when an image, video or story circulates rapidly

vortex (plural **vortices**) something flowing around an axis

wind field three-dimensional pattern of winds

wind-up radio radio powered by a clockwork mechanism that is wound up by hand

Find out more

Hurricane Sandy's brief and devastating impact only took place a short time ago. But already a vast amount has been written about it, and there is also an enormous amount of images and video footage. Here is a short selection of useful sources.

Books

Hurricanes (Eyewitness Disaster), Angela Royston (Franklin Watts, 2011)

Hurricanes and Tornadoes (Natural Disasters), Richard and Louise Spilsbury (Wayland, 2010)

Inside Hurricanes (Inside Series), Mary Kay Carson (Sterling, 2010)

The Superstorm Hurricane Sandy (True Books: Disasters), Josh Gregory (Scholastic, 2013)

Surviving Hurricanes (Children's True Stories: Natural Disasters), Elizabeth Raum (Raintree, 2012)

Films

Hurricane Heroes (2008)
This is a moving film about the rescue of 50,000 dogs, cats and other pets left behind after Hurricane Katrina.

Hurricanes! History's Most Destructive Storms (1995)
This documentary has amazing historic footage of some of the most devastating storms to have hit the United States, including Hurricanes Camille and Betsy.

The Perfect Storm (2000)
This is a thrilling adventure based on a true story, set during the monster "perfect" storm of 1991.

Storms, Cyclones and Hurricanes (2007)
This animated documentary shows how storms develop and behave.

Websites

www.bbc.co.uk/schools/gcsebitesize/geography/weather_climate/
weather_human_activity_rev1.shtml
Find out more about hurricanes, including Hurricane Katrina, on this website.

eo.ucar.edu/webweather/hurricanehome.html
This is a wide-ranging weather website for younger readers.

www.hurricanehunters.com
This is the home site for the Hurricane Hunters aircraft units.

www.livescience.com/24380-hurricane-sandy-status-data.html
This site provides facts about the superstorm, Hurricane Sandy.

www.metoffice.gov.uk/weather/tropicalcyclone/2012/sandy
This site explains all about tropical storms.

www.nasa.gov/mission_pages/hurricanes/archives/2012/h2012_Sandy.html
This NASA site gives a detailed timeline for Hurricane Sandy, including
satellite images of the storm.

www.nasa.gov/mission_pages/hurricanes/main/index.html#.UhcrfkxwbIU
This NASA site provides the latest news and historical archives about
worldwide tropical storms.

news.bbc.co.uk/cbbcnews/hi/newsid_4020000/newsid_4022100/4022129.
stm
This BBC website has an animated guide to hurricanes and lots of other
information about extreme weather systems.

More topics to research

1. Have there been big storms in your local area? For example, the UK has
   been hit by severe weather systems in 1953, 1987 and 2014.

2. What kind of new flood defences are being built? What measures are
   being taken to prevent disastrous flooding in vulnerable places around the
   world, such as in Mississippi, USA, and Bangladesh?

3. Follow a hurricane season. You can get regular updates on weather
   systems during a season from the National Hurricane Center site at
   www.nhc.noaa.gov.

4. Find out more about major cyclones throughout history, such as the 1881
   Haiphong typhoon in Vietnam, or the 1900 Galveston hurricane.

Index